Open Our Hearts

Daily prayers for Lent and Holy Week

Ann Gerondelis

To my family
John, Stacy and Isa
You teach me the power of love that stretches
Every day

Open Our Hearts

Daily prayers for Lent and Holy Week

Ann Gerondelis

wild goose
publications

www.ionabooks.com

Published 2018 by
Wild Goose Publications, 21 Carlton Court, Glasgow G5 9JP, UK,
the publishing division of the Iona Community.
Scottish Charity No. SC003794. Limited Company Reg. No. SC096243.

ISBN 978-1-84952-619-7

We gratefully acknowledge the contribution of the Drummond Trust,
3 Pitt Terrace, Stirling, towards the publication of this book

Overseas distribution
Australia: Willow Connection Pty Ltd, Unit 4A, 3–9 Kenneth Road, Manly Vale, NSW 2093
New Zealand: Pleroma, Higginson Street, Otane 4170, Central Hawkes Bay
Canada: Bayard Distribution, 10 Lower Spadina Ave., Suite 400, Toronto, Ontario M5V 2Z

Printed by Charlesworth Press, Wakefield, UK

Introduction

It's a miracle, really. That we who are embodied in this world are able to converse with the divine. Not only is God still speaking to us, but we can perceive God's presence in our midst, and respond. This is the miracle of prayer – this cyclical practice that invites us to commune with God and the world, and to bear witness to powerful transformation in the process. How grateful we are for this gift!

The devotions that follow are structured to support holy conversation through a regular pattern of listening to God's timeless love for the world.[1] The sketches and prayers are the result of a practice of drawing and writing in dialogue with scripture readings. This process opens up the texts, surfaces new perspectives and brings God's word to life. The result is a series of interwoven readings, prayers and images that invite reflection through each day of Lent and Holy Week.

A range of drawing methods were used to explore the biblical texts. Sometimes the drawings resulted from a series of intentional movements inspired by the scriptures. The drawing exploring the story of Mary at Jesus' feet resulted from gestural movements Mary might have made as she washed his feet with her hair. A billowing robe celebrates the movement of a father so eager to greet his prodigal son. In another drawing, God's all-encompassing love is embodied through multiple circular movements that translate to a deep, inviting visual space.

Other drawings invite engagement with the Bible to surface new understandings. The psalmist's description of the shadow of God's wing is reimagined as a space of splendour and joy. Abram's land and rivers emerge not simply as holy lands on an ancient map but as embodied environments navigated and embraced by God's people.

Christians claim Sunday as a sabbath day, yet Sunday is often the time when we are most distinctly divided into different 'types' of people of God, with neighbours attending separate houses of worship. *Open Our Hearts* invites us into a Sunday practice that explores our connections across faith traditions. The sketches and prayers for Sunday call us to celebrate those practices we hold in common, and which remind us of God's inclusive love for all God's people – and our collective call to feed the hungry, work for peace and build communities of love.

I pray that these pages open up space for you to meet God anew in these holy days. May word and image draw you into communion with God's abiding love and its transformative power to make all things new. Enjoy revisiting these pages in other seasons as well, as they invite you into God's holy presence and help us all to open our hearts and imagine together a more inclusive way to live as God's people.

Ann Gerondelis

1. Scripture quotations are from the New Revised Standard Version Bible, copyright © 1989 the Division of Christian Education of the National Council of the Churches of Christ in the United States of America. Used by permission. All rights reserved. Readings mostly follow the Evangelical Lutheran Church in America's Lectionary for the Lenten Season, Year C.

Contents

But it is God who establishes us with you in Christ and has anointed us …

2 Corinthians 1:21 (NRSV)

How grateful we are, O God,
that you call us,
that you claim us,
and that you mysteriously mark us in love.
We, your people – grateful indeed.

Amen

called

… Return to the Lord, your God,
for he is gracious and merciful,
slow to anger,
and abounding in steadfast love …

Joel 2:13 (NRSV)

O God, you call out to us in many ways.
Today, may we hear you,
see you
and know you are near,
saying: 'Come to me. All of you. Come.'

Amen

See the animation of the drawing here:
https://bit.ly/2GR8TW6

… the same Lord is Lord of all …

Romans 10:12 (NRSV)

Friday Week 1

gathered

O God, gather us together
and help us to become
a community of your people,
called to love.

Amen

... and he brought us into this place
and gave us this land,
a land flowing with milk and honey.

Deuteronomy 26:9 (NRSV)

Saturday Week 1

given

O generous God,
transform us in these Lenten days,
that we may be gifts of love to one another.
For there is enough for all.
Enough food.
Enough money.
Love overflowing.

Amen

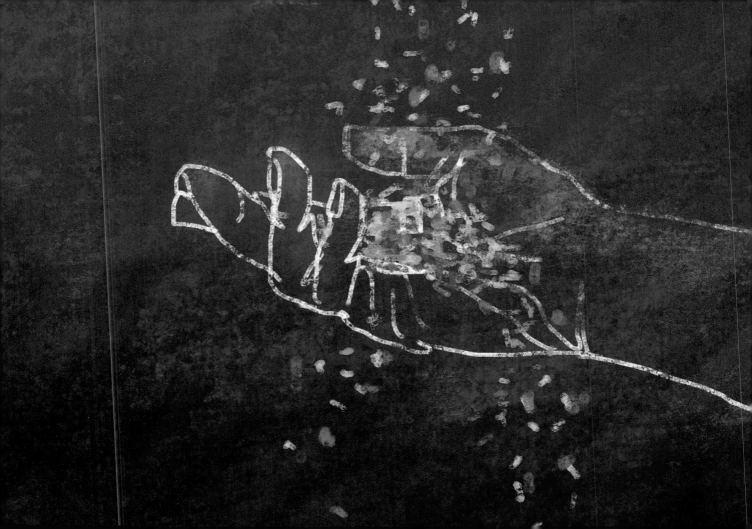

holy

On these sabbath days, dear God,
how miraculous it must be
to hear all of your children praying.
On mats; in homes, standing and kneeling beside beds;
in cathedrals, temples and mosques;
in the Arctic and in the tropics;
in the light and in the dark …
Silently and loudly,
in happiness and in sorrow, so many call to you.
May we find joy in joining in the chorus
with all your holy people –
longing to be fed, working for peace,
reaching out to build communities of love.
Together we praise you.

Amen

*Sunday is a day that often moves us in different directions
and divides us most distinctly into different kinds of God's
people. On these days, we pause to celebrate our common
faith practices and claim them as holy.*

connected

He brought him outside and said,
'Look toward heaven and count the stars,
if you are able to count them.'
Then he said to him, 'So shall your descendants be.'

Genesis 15:5 (NRSV)

O God, our birth in this world
is one of your countless creative acts
in your ever-evolving creation.
Help us to step back and see
the larger whole we are part of.
We are not, after all, islands,
but more like constellations,
deeply connected to you,
to our past and future, and to one another.
Help us shine together
and become what you dream we can be.

Amen

On that day the Lord made a covenant with Abram,
saying, 'To your descendants I give this land,
from the river of Egypt to the great river,
the river Euphrates …'

Genesis 15:18 (NRSV)

Tuesday Week 2

covenant

O generous God, in covenant, you bind us to you,
to each other and to the earth
and all the promise it holds.
Open our eyes to the potential
embedded within this covenant relationship.
It's hard to imagine
that all that surrounds us
came from your gift of land and rivers.
It has become for us machines and medicines,
fences and Fortran,
elevators and election seasons,
and oh so much more.

Be in our creating.
May our imaginations be fed
by this covenant relationship with you
and with all your people.
May the work of our hearts and hands
be deemed good, for the life of the world.

Amen

cry

Hear, O Lord, when I cry aloud,
be gracious to me and answer me!

Psalm 27:7 (NRSV)

O God, your Spirit deeply connects us to you
and to each other.
Potential surrounds us.
Yet, we are struck by news of pain,
separation and injustice –
day after day, hour after hour.
How do we respond
to the unrelenting horrors we call the news?
God, help us not grow silently numb
to pain and suffering –
or become eager to hear the latest.
Build us into a people
who authentically
and courageously
cry in pain.

May the beautiful sounds of your church
also include those
who passionately name injustice and suffering,
and cry 'No!'
And may the voices of your people echo
in chambers of justice around the world.

Amen

baptised

But our citizenship is in heaven,
and it is from there that we are expecting a Saviour,
the Lord Jesus Christ.

Philippians 3:20 (NRSV)

O God, remind each of us this day
that we are beautifully human
and beautifully holy (at least a bit).

Love,
Your beloved children with wet foreheads

Amen

Teach me your way, O Lord,
and lead me on a level path …

Psalm 27:11(NRSV)

O God, some days it seems
we are moving between two very different worlds –
one right side up, the other upside down.
We are in, then we are out.
We give and we take.
We break and are broken.
We follow your call,
drawing us in and sending us out.
In and out. In and out.
In the process, might you be slowly making us new?
Remind us today
of your constant love and grace
that accompanies us and supports our walk
through the thresholds before us.
Let it be so, O creative God. Let it be so indeed.

Amen

Friday Week 2

between

See the animation of the drawing here:
https://bit.ly/2s6ipQM

dazzling

And while he was praying,
the appearance of his face changed,
and his clothes became dazzling white.

Luke 9:29 (NRSV)

We've seen it, God.
Your dazzling light radiating from the faces
of so many of your people.
How you live today through their love and witness!
May your gifts of love and light
continue to break into even our darkest places
and creatively connect all that separates us,
one from another, us from you.
Lit by your love, may we work together
to become that brilliant Beloved Community
that you dream we can be.
Let it be so.

Amen

holy

O God, how is it even possible
that we can speak and listen to you,
that we can imagine crossing the threshold
between sacred and profane?
How miraculous it is that we understand
even a glimpse of your holiness.
You are bigger than we can ever name or imagine.
You are mystery. You are love.
You are grace upon grace.

Today, as we process in worship,
we ask that you join our steps
with those of your holy people in Bali, Indonesia,
and all around the world,
longing to be fed, working for peace,
reaching out to build communities of love.
Together we praise you.

Amen

ho

Ho, everyone who thirsts, come to the waters;
and you that have no money, come, buy and eat!
Come, buy wine and milk without money and without price.

Isaiah 55:1 (NRSV)

Ho. Now that's an interruption you don't hear every day!
Thanks for this, God.
Your call should be one that stops us and reminds us
of how counter-cultural your invitation is.
Ho. We're not used to stopping now, are we?
We've got things to do!
Ho. Everyone is included?
But surely you don't mean 'them'.
Ho. My place at the table isn't earned?
Shoulder to shoulder with these
who don't even know how to show proper respect?
Ho. Even our deepest hungers will be fed?
I don't even know what they are.

Keep the interruptions coming, God.
Today, may I practise trusting
where you lead me.

Amen

Incline your ear, and come to me;
listen, so that you may live …

Isaiah 55:3 (NRSV)

Earbuds. Full schedules.
Talking heads on screens surround us.
It's no wonder that we have a hard time
hearing your still small voice, dear God.
It's easy to get lulled into the belief
that our perspective on life is quite fine as it is.
'We got this!' 'Things could be worse, after all. Right?'

In the midst of our illusions of independence,
we ask that you keep whispering to us.
And shout when you need to.
Draw us back to that voice we know:
the one that calls us back to a holy way.
The one where love matters – more than anything.
Be patient with us. We need to practise.
Help us today.

Tuesday Week 3

listen

Incline our ear
that we might hear your call anew,
and be filled
with hope and wonder, once again.

Amen

expand

For my thoughts are not your thoughts,
nor are your ways my ways, says the Lord.

Isaiah 55:8 (NRSV)

We long to know you, God.
We attempt descriptions in image and word
so that we might understand
a bit more of the grand mystery of you.
Yet too often our descriptions
limit our understanding of you
and all that you dream for us.
Help us, in this Lenten season,
to see the world as you do –
an expanded view with mercies
wider than we can imagine
and love deeper than any we know.
May our anxieties fade
as we practise loving
more broadly and generously.

Love us in this process, O God.
Open our hearts and weave us together
as one people of God,
eager to discover all that you imagine
for this wide and wonderful world you love.

Amen

open

So I will bless you as long as I live;
I will lift up my hands and call on your name.

Psalm 63:4 (NRSV)

Clenched. Full. Wrung.
Some days
those are the best descriptions
of my hand positions.
Does that say something about
how I'm in dialogue with the world around me?
Likely so.
What if, instead, I imagined
that this is the time
when I am called to open my hands,
to empty them, and to place them
in the presence of unceasing love and grace.
What would that do for this time and this place?
What would it do for me?
Worth an experiment.

God, grant me courage today
to open my hands to new possibilities.
To you.
Blow, Spirit. Blow …

Amen

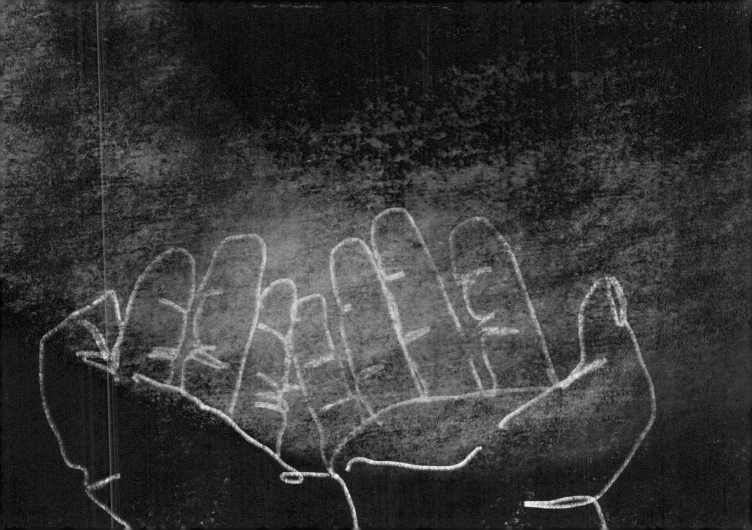

joy

… for you have been my help,
and in the shadow of your wings I sing for joy.

Psalm 63:7 (NRSV)

We are not alone.
When we call (and when we don't) you are here.
O God, how miraculous that you come so close,
breathing in and through us.
We see you in hands and feet
bringing grace and mercy.
And sometimes we catch a gorgeous glimpse of you.
Care all-encompassing. Love far reaching.
Speaking in many voices.
Sweeping across boundaries. No one excluded.
We stand in awe.

Under your wing, we see the possibility
of your people gathered together.
Under your wing, we see the gifts we each bring.
Under your wing, we see an image of a loving community
whose strength grows from our beautiful differences.

Under your wing, we move together in love.
Eyes filled with wonder.
Let it be so, dear gathering God.
Let it be so.

Amen

He replied, 'Sir, let it alone for one more year,
until I dig around it and put manure on it.'

Luke 13:8 (NRSV)

Some days, we're not sure why
we're called to this time and place –
especially when we see
such abuse and injustice around us.
At times like these, dear God, remind us that
even in the midst of fear and pain –
sometimes *especially* in the midst of fear and pain –
you creatively give birth to new life.
In this time and place, may we bloom.
Do not let anxieties keep us silent
but energised to love.
Right where we find ourselves planted.
And may we take our call
to be courageous and vocal stewards seriously:
working to encourage others
who share our soil,

Saturday Week 3

bloom

and nurturing and tending to these,
our neighbours.
May we live believing
that fruit and flower grow
from your observant tending
and generous, patient love.
For the life of the world that you love.

Amen

Today's sketch is of a blooming fig flower.

holy

O God, how gracious you are,
in dialogue with all who call your name.
We come humbly, and boldly,
with confidence and fear.
We sing. We cry. We write. We wail.
And in response, always, you speak.

Today, as we call out your name,
join our voices with those of your holy people
in the Middle East,
and all around the world,
longing to be fed,
working for peace,
reaching out to build communities of love.
Together we praise you.

Amen

Therefore let all who are faithful offer prayer to you;
at a time of distress, the rush of mighty waters
shall not reach them.

Psalm 32:6 (NRSV)

Pain that continues day after day.
Hunger that renders us immobile.
Fear that gives birth to isolation and hate.
Frustration that grows into anger.
Deep sorrow and regret.
Guilt that won't let go.
Power that cripples.
From these, and all that causes distress for your children,
we ask for your deliverance, O God.

Amen

Monday Week 4
deliverance

See the animation of the drawing here:
https://bit.ly/2KVbOPQ

light

Be glad in the Lord and rejoice, O righteous,
and shout for joy, all you upright in heart.

Psalm 32:11 (NRSV)

And sometimes, dear God,
the light breaks through –
and all is transformed.
The darkness remains, but somehow it seems
to live in service to the light.
How grateful we are
for surprising transformations,
for your persistent light
which knows no boundaries.
May we practise stepping aside
and giving the light space to dance,
light and love opening up new perspectives,
and changing the world.

Amen

So if anyone is in Christ, there is a new creation:
everything old has passed away;
see, everything has become new!

2 Corinthians 5:17 (NRSV)

Wednesday Week 4

new

Emails and to-do lists, appointments and repairs,
and then there are relationships to tend to.
Some days the complexity of life can overwhelm us.
It's easy to lose sight of love.
It doesn't have to be like this.
Open our eyes to new perspectives, dear God.
Help us to see potential in the midst of our mess.
Let us boldly believe,
and graciously make way for your new creation.
Let it be so!

Amen

And the Pharisees and the scribes were grumbling and saying,
'This fellow welcomes sinners and eats with them.'

Luke 15:2 (NRSV)

welcome

God, we gather around tables to work,
to exchange ideas,
to eat together.
We sit at tables to share,
to empathise,
or to dominate.
Make us mindful of who's around the table with us,
and who is not.
Widen our welcome when our sights are limited.

Today may we use time and space
to make room for voices different from our own.
Let us not default to taking sides,
but may our exchange and dialogue
build a new spectrum of understanding.

May we welcome your invitation
to make room for love, for light,
and a bit of laughter.
May love grow from our gatherings this day.

Amen

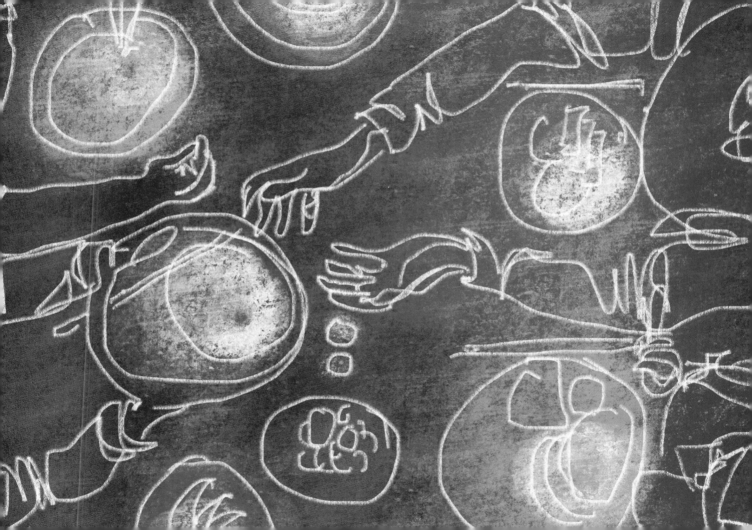

share

The younger of them said to his father, 'Father,
give me the share of the property that will belong to me.'
So he divided his property between them.

Luke 15:12 (NRSV)

It might be easier if we were a nomadic people,
taking up residency only temporarily in a place,
then gathering up our limited possessions
and moving on to the next.
But we love our stuff.
We know what is ours and what is theirs.
And we usually pay pretty close attention
to whose stuff is 'better'.
Remind us of the joy of being generous, dear God.
Of pooling our resources, dividing and sharing.
May we become a forgiving people who choose,
again and again,
to collectively share resources.
How counter-cultural is that!
What a sign of love.

Amen

So he set off and went to his father.
But while he was still far off, his father saw him
and was filled with compassion;
he ran and put his arms around him and kissed him.

Luke 15:20 (NRSV)

Saturday Week 4

found

Throughout our days and nights, dear God, we often get lost.
Sometimes for years, sometimes for decades,
we find ourselves wandering.
Disconnected. Confused. Alone.
And then, hope comes.
In so many different ways, you call us back,
and remind us that we are loved and cherished.
How grateful we are.
May we extend your love and grace this day,
generously welcoming each and every one of your children
who turns, looking for love.
Let us see your light shining within them
and meet them with arms wide open.
Wide open indeed.

Amen

holy

O God, how beautiful to be marked and claimed as yours.
Today we thank you for our Hindu friends
and their tradition of forehead-marking.
This practice often closes their morning prayer,
reminding them that they are yours.
The *tilak* U shape represents the lotus feet of God,
and the red *chandlo* represents the individual,
bowing at God's feet.
When devotees see the *tilak chandlo* of others
throughout the day,
they are reminded of their own, and others', sacred calling.

May we remember, on this Sabbath day,
that you call us to be your collective hands and feet
in this wide and wonderful world that you love.
May we work together
through rich and varied holy practices
to become the Beloved Community that you dream we can be.
One holy people of God.

Amen

trust

I am about to do a new thing;
now it springs forth, do you not perceive it?
I will make a way in the wilderness
and rivers in the desert.

Isaiah 43:19 (NRSV)

You invite us into the wilderness, dear God.
But the way ahead looks so uncertain.
How do we take that first step?
I hear the invitation.
I see the potential, at least a bit of it.
But this is a place so different than the ones I know.
Where I stand, might rules.
Positions matter.
I know what is mine.
But a step into the wilderness?
All bets are off.
What rules this place? … Really.
Grace? Love? Mercy?
How does extravagant love work?

What are you dreaming up in the days ahead?
May I trust you, as I gently step in.
Walking together.
Becoming.

Amen

The wild animals will honour me,
the jackals and the ostriches;
for I give water in the wilderness,
rivers in the desert,
to give drink to my chosen people …

Isaiah 43:20 (NRSV)

Today, dear God, may we gratefully join the chorus
of all who pull their head out of the sand
to look around and say:
'Well … Wow. Amazing. Thanks God!'
Together, let us celebrate that we are all creatures –
strange, wise and wonderful –
being made by you.
Squawk! Thanks be to God.

Amen

Tuesday Week 5

squawk!

dream

When the Lord restored the fortunes of Zion,
we were like those who dream.

Psalm 126:1 (NRSV)

From a 2nd-grade desk by the window
to a bench in an ancient temple, we dream.
Oh, do we dream. We dream of tomorrows yet to come,
of coming out on top, of having enough.
But how wonderful it would be
if we could dream together.
What if we could float our hopes for the future
and collectively keep them aloft?
My actions supporting their dreams.
Theirs supporting mine.
All of us working together.
Delighting in the joy of realising the dreams
of all God's children.

As we make plans for our communities, dear God,
help us to loft our own dreams,

and also to stand back and marvel
at the colourful possibilities of the dreams of others.
May we work to keep them aloft,
knowing that you dream great things for us –
communities of peace and grace and mercy.
Spaces of extravagant love
for each and every one of your people.
Today, may we believe in your promises –
and dream big. So big. For all.

Amen

*May those who sow in tears
reap with shouts of joy.*

Psalm 126:5 (NRSV)

tears

Rolling down the cheeks of a mother
waking in a refugee camp
to the sound of her crying child.
Pouring from the eyes of a woman,
abused and fearful,
unable to find refuge in her own home.
So many tears. Collectively, so many.
Is it possible that they add up to something?

O God, we ask that you collect the tears
of your people around the world.
Help us to see in them
a glistening hope for a brighter tomorrow.
May they grow into puddles, ponds and lakes
that speak of possibility,
and power in numbers.

And may our brothers and sisters
whose cheeks are wet this day
know that you cry with them, and with us all.
Creating pools of love.

Amen

Beloved, I do not consider that I have made it my own;
but this one thing I do:
forgetting what lies behind
and straining forward to what lies ahead …

Philippians 3:13 (NRSV)

On some days it's easier to see the fruits of our labours.
On other days, it feels like hours of toiling with little return.
Help us on the tough days, O God.
So many work on our streets
sowing seeds of peace and justice.
But their seedlings are often and easily trampled.
Give your good-seed-sowers the support they need,
and a glimpse – every now and then –
of the glorious golden fields of harvest
that are only possible because of their efforts.
Bless your sowers near and far
and the work they do with you.

Amen

Today's sketch features a regendered Oklahoma Sooner
in her imagined golden fields.

extravagant

Mary took a pound of costly perfume made of pure nard,
anointed Jesus' feet, and wiped them with her hair.
The house was filled with the fragrance of the perfume.

John 12:3 (NRSV)

Today, dear God,
as we read of Mary's anointing of Jesus' feet,
we are struck by her full-body engagement.
How hungry she is to see, to feel, to smell,
to be fully immersed in the presence of her Saviour –
of Love Incarnate.
May we, in this Lenten season, grow so hungry for you
that we drop our defences and say YES to love like Mary.
Extravagant love that immerses all our senses.
Love that flows unceasingly for all.
Love now – even when hate surrounds us.
Love that spreads miraculously from person to person,
that fills the rooms of our homes,
our neighbourhoods and cities.

O God, when violence grows around us,
it seems impossible to dream of love.
Be love in us now.
Be love in all your people.
May we be bearers of extravagant love
in a world that so desperately needs it.
All in! No matter the cost.
For love. All in!

Amen

O God, be with the many hands around the world this day –
those who count your blessings,
and those who whisper pains.
Around and around in a chain uniting heaven and earth,
may our longings be woven with those of every time and place.

May blessings beyond number abound
for your people around the world,
longing to be fed,
working for peace,
reaching out to build communities of love.
Together we praise you.

Amen

holy

This is the day that the Lord has made;
let us rejoice and be glad in it.

Psalm 118:24 (NRSV)

Monday Week 6

unfolding

It's not like this.
No, the Atlanta, Georgia skyline is currently surrounded
by a blanket of black.
It's the season when we shift our clocks an hour ahead
for daylight savings time.
We lose an hour of sleep and waken to dark skies.
This makes for a sleepy Monday morning.
It's a rocky start, to be sure,
but we know you are making this day too, dear God.

So, this morning I sketch my dreams for a glorious day into reality.
And I pray: God, fill us with the hope of the day unfolding
and all the potential you know that it holds.
What gifts you give to all your people.
Extraordinary gifts indeed.

Amen

Blessed is the one who comes in the name of the Lord …

Psalm 118:26 (NRSV)

come

How miraculous it is, dear God,
that you walked on the earth as Jesus.
How miraculous also that, in the midst of the chaos,
Jesus was recognised and celebrated as yours!
Your people stopped what they were doing,
went to the Mount of Olives
and collectively organised a space for God's love to enter.
Eyes on the path. Ears tuned to the blessed One.

What guides our attention these days, dear God?
Where do we frame our view?
And what words are we taking time to listen to?
How do we turn away from what is not holy,
and make space for love?

In the midst of the chaos,
may we, this week, make time to turn away,
to turn to you,
to frame our eyes on the sacred,
making space for love.
Come, O blessed One.
Be love in our streets,
our homes,
our hearts.

Amen

waken

… Morning by morning he wakens –
wakens my ear to listen as those who are taught.

Isaiah 50:4 (NRSV)

Gorgeous harmonies,
boiling test tubes,
kindnesses spoken,
cries of lament,
shouts for justice.
Your voice is certainly still speaking around us, God!
Sounds we hear daily remind us of your constant work –
creating, redeeming and sanctifying.

Awaken our ears today,
that we might hear your voice anew:
creating conversations that turn towards love
when anger is the easier option;
redeeming lives and restoring hope;
sanctifying people and places
that seem anything but holy sometimes.

Remind us this day
how beloved we are in your sight,
called to be love in places that need a bit more.
Let it be so this day, dear God.
Let it be so.

Amen

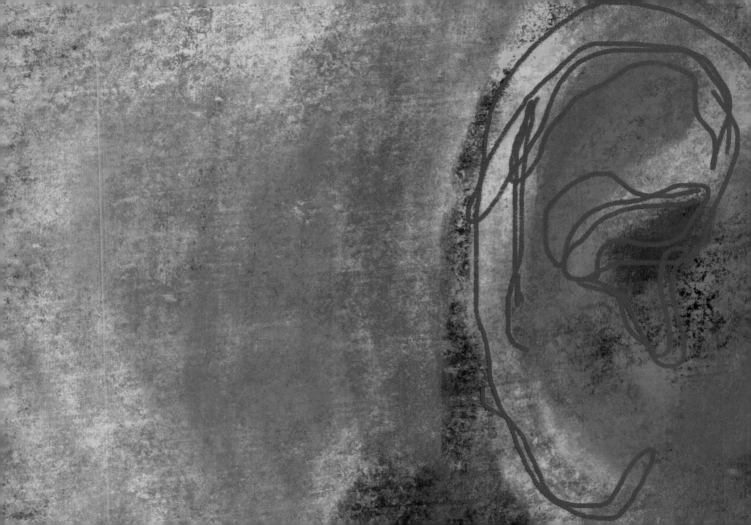

steadfast

… I have set my face like flint,
and I know that I shall not be put to shame …

Isaiah 50:7 (NRSV)

Hold fast. Steady. Don't rock it.
Maybe we can learn a thing or two from sailors at sea.
Sailors seem to be ones
who constantly battle with exterior forces.
Wave after wave comes crashing,
and throughout the storm, they watch, listen and respond.
Watch, listen and respond.

In the midst of things that we know
will be rocking our boats in the days ahead, dear God,
we ask that you help us to hold fast.
Help us when it's hard to lift our heads,
to watch, listen and respond in love.
And when the next wave comes,
help us to do it all again, with love and grace.
One day at a time.

Remind us that your love is steadfast,
and your arms are outstretched
for every single one of your children,
each created in your image.
Born to love.

Amen

… but emptied himself, taking the form of a slave,
being born in human likeness …

Philippians 2:7 (NRSV)

empty

Boy, do we love to be full.
Full stomachs. Heads full of ideas.
Full pews where we worship.
Houses full of stuff to meet every need.

In the midst of our longings for fullness, dear God,
we ask that you open our hearts to the gift of emptiness.
May we long for space that allows us,
actually forces us,
to see in new ways –
to see you, ourselves and our relationships differently.
Space that invites us to see what we are becoming,
especially those parts of us
that we don't really want to explore.

Space that invites us
to see you at work in the world around us.
Space that opens up
for gentle light and transforming love
that has been there all along,
persistently waiting to be invited in.
May we courageously begin
the spiritual work of emptying ourselves.
For you.

Amen

love

Let the same mind be in you that was in Christ Jesus …

Philippians 2:5 (NRSV)

In so many ways, we visibly speak our minds.
By who we befriend, by how we spend our money,
by the volume of our voices,
by where we go Sunday mornings,
by how we vote.
Might it be possible, as our holiest week approaches,
to also visibly speak of love?

It might mean creating a bit more space for listening,
instead of conversations filled
with recollections of others' ghastly actions.
It might mean taking time to invite in
those who see things differently,
rather than time strategising
how to achieve our own goals.
It might mean pausing
to hear the needs and longings

of one who is down and out,
instead of averting our gaze and walking away.
This will take some work.
Some time.
Some practice.
It might take a whole Holy Week.
Thank heavens one approaches.

Amen

Palm Sunday

holy

O God, what a gift it is to discover ways
of entering into sacred time and space –
to get a hint of that thin place
where earth and heaven meet.
To prepare ourselves,
we raise our voices in song and prayer,
we occupy spaces set apart,
we take on different postures
and clothe ourselves in sacred garments.
In doing so we all look and sound quite different.

On this Sabbath day,
remind us of how similar we are,
and the power that we hold as your people.
Clothe Buddhist monks and all your children
with enlightenment,
that we may work together
to build communities of love and tender grace.
O God of peace, let it be so.

Amen

For I will pass through the land of Egypt that night …

Exodus 12:12 (NRSV)

O most gracious God, if only we could mark
places where your love and mercy are needed –
where people find themselves in situations
they could never have imagined
and cannot see any way out of.
If only we could make a sign
asking you to watch over them,
to bring them safety and protection from danger.
Freedom from the things that enslave them.

What doors would we mark?
Places of abuse where many are dehumanised.
Places of war where so many
are forced to become refugees.
Places where people must work for low wages.
So many suffer in our midst, dear God.
We name these people now,
and ask that you keep them safe from harm …

Monday Holy Week

mercy

In this Holy Week,
may we be about the business
of making visible signs in the world around us.
Signs that declare your mercy and love
for all your people.
Let us continue to be declarers of your love
for each and every one,
and let us rejoice in discovering together
what it means to be called one people of God.
Free to love and serve.

Amen

… You have loosed my bonds.

Psalm 116:16 (NRSV)

Tuesday Holy Week

unbound

I haven't taken enough psychology classes
to know why we have this fear of change,
even change that loosens our shackles a bit.
Somehow, our fear of the unknown
keeps us bound to unhealthy habits,
relationships, self-identities, career paths.
What if we were to really listen
to hear what we know to be true –
that you promise spaces of love and mercy
for all of your people?
Grace upon grace for each of us.

May we lean into this promise in the days ahead.
May we truly consider the notion
that you have called us to this time and place –
spaces already overflowing

with milk and honey,
with goodness
we have only caught a glimpse of.
May we courageously listen to your call,
letting the ropes fall
as we walk into new possibilities.
A new heaven and a new earth indeed!

Amen

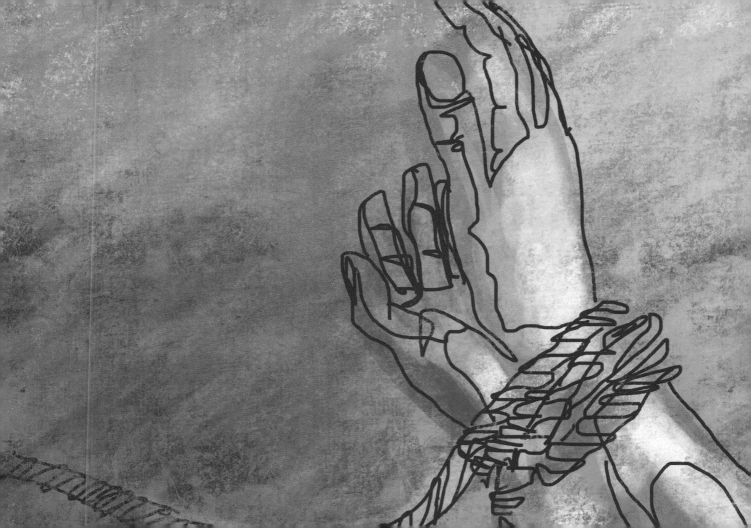

All we like sheep have gone astray;
we have all turned to our own way …

Isaiah 53:6 (NRSV)

Handel's delightful melody of
'All we like sheep have gone astray'
rings in my head,
making it sound like true delight
to wander 'ah-straay-ay-AY-ay-ay-AY-ay-AY …'

So today I sketch and pray to pull myself around.
What if, dear God, we explore ways
of bringing your gifts of love and grace
to the world in an intentional way?
What if we realign ourselves
and name and claim what you are calling us to do?
What if we aim to posture ourselves
as your full-frontal sheep?!
Embracing our gifts,
we might plant ourselves front and centre
where love and grace are most needed –

Wednesday Holy Week
full-frontal

in our homes and workplaces.
Where is full-frontal love *not* needed?
What if we were all in? Really in.
All in for love, even when it's hard.
All in for grace, when judgement is easier.
All in for you.

This week, may we find joy in placing ourselves
where you have been leading us
to stand firm for love.
Love that wins every time.
May we be your full-frontal sheep,
delightfully immovable,
and maybe even with a bit of attitude.
Baaa!

Amen

blessed

Very truly, I tell you,
servants are not greater than their master,
nor are messengers greater than the one who sent them.

John 13:16 (NRSV)

It's awkward, right?
Kneeling down,
grabbing the heavy pitcher dripping with water,
and the bowl big enough for feet.
Then there's the towel – don't want that to fall in the
water. It's nice and soft, but a bit bulky
now that I'm trying to coordinate everything.
Then, oh my, I am so in this person's personal space!
I mean, communion is shoulder to shoulder,
but I've barely met this friend,
and we're so close right now we can smell each other.
I'll wait down here; first one shoe, then the sock.
Nice argyles, btw.
Here, let me help you balance a bit. There you go.
Now, how does this work again? Left first, there you go.
Now the other one. Uh huh. Nice and dry now.

There we are. Let me just move this aside.
A big hug. Peace. Wow.
That was love. And feet were washed.
Messy. Humbling.
What a reminder
that this building-communities-of-love thing
is a full-contact sport.
May every awkward, messy, smelly,
love-filled full-contact encounter,
and all the missteps that go along with them,
be blessed. So very blessed indeed.
May we meet you anew this day,
in the midst of it all.

Amen

Above all, maintain constant love for one another …

1 Peter 4:8 (NRSV)

Good Friday

here

Abe Lincoln slept here. Even better – Elvis did.
What makes us love to hear these stories?
Maybe their concreteness in time and place
helps us to reimagine what is possible
for ourselves here and now.
A bit of tangible hope perhaps.

In these days when physical lines are being drawn
between people, between communities,
between countries,
it's so easy to lose our confidence,
to lose sight of hope, of love.
Today we hear again the story of Golgotha.
Oh, what a time. Oh, what a place.
But here, tangible hope. Here, love reimagined.

O dear God,
who claims people and places again and again,
claim us now.

Claim our streets, our communities,
our countries, our planet and more.
For love. Claim us. Claim them. Claim here.
Claim yesterday.
Claim all the tomorrows yet to come.
Then, claimed as yours,
may we walk into our heres and nows,
and confidently be love anew.
May our hands and feet
be part of love's unfolding story where we are.
Now. Today.
May love happen here.
Because of you.

Amen

And the curtain of the temple
was torn in two,
from top to bottom.

Mark 15:38 (NRSV)

It is finished.

Amen

Holy Saturday

tetelestai

Make a joyful noise to the Lord, all the earth;
break forth into joyous song and sing praises.

Psalm 98:4 (NRSV)

Easter Sunday

alleluia

On this night, we gathered,
we waited and watched.
Our stories were woven together
with those of your saints of every time and every place.
On this night, earth met heaven.
On this night, humanity met divinity.
And your love, dear God, dawned anew,
stretching out for all your people.

We pray that your love is born again in our hearts,
our homes, our cities
and in all countries around the world.

With gratitude, we sing Alleluia!
May a new day dawn for us all. Alleluia indeed!

Amen

O beloved one,
whose face glows with the light of Easter,
you bear the mark of God,
born for this time
and this place.

May God grant you courage
as you walk into the brilliant dawn.
For in your open hands and heart
you will see God.

You journey not alone,
but with the power of God's people near and far,
working together to build a world
of justice and mercy.

Know today
that the love of the risen Christ shines through you
and through the hearts and hands of all of God's people.
Indeed, it is changing the world.

Christ is risen.
He is risen indeed.
Alleluia!

blessing

See the animation of the drawing here:
https://bit.ly/2IL2jCo